Sound Trackers

1970s Pop

Brunning, Bob
1970s pop. – (Sound trackers)
1. Popular music – 1971-1980 – Juvenile literature
I. Title
781. 6 ' 4' 09047

Printed and bound in Italy.

INTRODUCTION

The 1970s were turbulent. The Vietnam war raged and there was political unrest all over the world. The UK joined the EEC. Margaret Thatcher became the first woman Prime Minister of Britain. US President, Richard Nixon, resigned in disgrace.

The Apollo flights to the moon ended. The supersonic Concorde service between London and New York began, as did Laker's walk-on walk-off airline.

Believed by many to be the greatest guitarist ever, Eric Clapton plays on in the 1990s.

On the music scene, many different kinds of bands and musicians achieved success. Punk music exploded, contrasting with the sophisticated music of bands like the Eagles and Fleetwood Mac. Many of the superstars of the '70s began their careers earlier. Van Morrison, Eric Clapton, Fleetwood Mac and Rod Stewart all had their roots in the UK's 'blues boom' which had erupted during the previous decade. David Bowie and the Sex Pistols could not have been more dissimilar, but they both presented a radical approach to their music, very different from the ethereal Procol Harum and the unashamedly commercial bands like the Bee Gees and Abba.

The music industry lost some major artists during the '70s. Elvis Presley died in 1977, the same year as glam rock star Marc Bolan of T. Rex. Other deaths included those of Jimi Hendrix, Jim Morrison, Gene Vincent, Sid Vicious and Keith Moon. As with many of their predecessors, some of these untimely deaths were related to drug or alcohol abuse.

ABBA

The already successful and accomplished Swedish group, unbelievably called Bjorn and Benny, Agnetha and Anni Frid, decided that their name was too much of a mouthful. They decided to use an acronym. The first letters of their four Christian names produced a much snappier title, ABBA. The four members were no newcomers to the pop scene when they joined forces in 1971. Agnetha Faltskog had had chart success in 1968 and Bjorn and Benny had worked together for some time on and off in various successful bands.

TRIBUTE BANDS
Imitation is the sincerest form of flattery, and there has been a development in the music industry over the last decade – tribute bands.

The Bootleg Beatles, the Strolling Bones, Fleetwood Back plus a dozen other bands perform their heroes' music – and make a good living doing so.

They generally do an excellent job and always demonstrate their knowledge of and affection for the classic bands they imitate. One of the most successful? Bjorn Again!

The ABBA lookalikes, Bjorn Again.

CAREER PLANS

Bjorn and Benny sometimes worked as session musicians and bumped into Agnetha and Anni. The four decided to combine their singing and writing talents. Abba wanted to be successful internationally. With Stig Anderson, their manager and producer, a business plan was devised. First stop, the Eurovision Song Contest.

Bjorn and Agnetha had three children together.

Benny and Anni got together in 1970 and divorced in '81.

Their second attempt won. 'Waterloo' was a magnificently produced song. It made No. 1 in six countries and was recorded in several languages to maximise sales.

HIT AFTER HIT AFTER HIT

Bjorn and Agnetha married, as did Benny and Anni. They toured extensively, used the media wisely and produced bouncy, commercial records. In the UK 15 singles made the Top 5, eight of them No. 1s. Their success was repeated all over the world. 'Mamma Mia' was No. 1 in Australia for ten weeks and stayed in the charts for two years. 'Dancing Queen' topped the charts in the USA, UK and eight other countries. Stig Anderson announced, " ... we are the most successful band in the world, because we have sold more records than anybody else, between 75,000,000 and 100,000,000 – more than the Beatles or Elvis Presley." In 1982 Abba were Sweden's biggest source of overseas earnings, beating Volvo and Ikea!

'Abba'
June '75
'Greatest Hits'
April '76
'The Album'
January '78

'Abba: The Collection : One'
September '87
'Abba: The Collection : Two'
November '88

ABBA SPLIT

The break-up of the couples' marriages led to ABBA's demise. All members were fabulously rich and all four developed creative solo careers. Bjorn and Benny notably teamed up with the UK's Tim Rice to produce the hit musical 'Chess' in London.

The BEE GEES

Widely recognised as one of Australia's best known musical exports, the Gibb brothers were not actually born there. Barry Gibb was born in Douglas, on the Isle of Man in 1946 and the twins, Robin and Maurice, were born in Manchester, England, in 1949. They all started performing at a very young age, making their first public appearance at the Gaumont Theatre in Manchester when the twins were just seven years old.

HEADING FOR THE BIG TIME

In 1958 the Gibb family emigrated to Australia. The brothers made a name for themselves as a harmony trio and had their own TV show. By 1962 they were signed to Australia's Festival record label. During the next four years, the Bee Gees released twelve singles. Three of them topped the Australian charts. Their first album in 1965, was called, amazingly, 'Barry Gibb And The Bee Gees Sing And Play Fourteen Barry Gibb Songs'!

The boys wanted to make it on the international music scene. In 1967, as their 13th single, 'Spicks and Specks' hit the top of the Australian charts, the Gibb brothers were on an aeroplane bound for London. They had an appointment with Robert Stigwood, a director of Beatles' manager Brian Epstein's company. He loved what he heard and quickly secured the Bee Gees a recording contract with Polydor.

The young trio appeared on TV every week.

The Bee Gees formed their band soon after their arrival in the UK.

GETTING THE ACT TOGETHER

The brothers recruited drummer Colin Peterson and guitarist Vince Melouney, both Australians living in London. Their single, 'New York Mining Disaster, 1941', entered the Top 20 on both sides of the Atlantic. Their first album did even better, making the Top 10 in the UK and USA. Later in 1967 'Massachusetts' gave the Bee Gees their first No. 1 hit while they were still teenagers! But cracks appeared within the band. The twins disagreed about the group's direction, Melouney left and alcohol and drug abuse, together with a 'rock star' lifestyle, took its toll. Robin left briefly; Peterson for good.

SATURDAY NIGHT FEVER

By 1973 the Bee Gees were playing the UK cabaret circuit. Their career lurched up again in 1975 with their US Top 10 hit, 'Nights On Broadway'. In 1977 their album 'Children Of The World' sold in truckloads and their singles hit the '70s disco scene just right. Their greatest success was nigh. Robert Stigwood asked them to write songs for a film, 'Saturday Night Fever'. The success of these songs was monumental. 'How Deep Is Your Love' stayed for 17 weeks at the top of the US 'Billboard' charts. The next two singles 'Stayin' Alive' and 'Night Fever' also made No. 1. The album sold 30,000,000 copies and won five trophies at the 1978 Grammy awards.

Still producing interesting work, the Bee Gees have made a huge and important contribution to the music scene over two decades.

DISCO FEVER

Discomania gripped the UK and USA during the '70s. Instead of hiring a band of musicians to play in a limited style, one DJ and a loud sound system could fill venues with customers who could dance to the latest records. DJs would programme the music to create an atmosphere.

The phenomenon was captured in a classic movie starring John Travolta. 'Saturday Night Fever' featured songs by the Bee Gees, Yvonne Elliman, KC and the Sunshine Band and more. 20 years on in 1998 it opened as a stage musical in London.

The movie captured the '70s disco mood.

'First'
July '67
'Odessa'
March '69
'Best Of The Bee Gees'
October '69

'Saturday Night Fever'
March '78
'Bee Gees Greatest'
October '79
'Staying Alive'
July '83

DAVID BOWIE

David Robert Jones was born on 8 January 1947 in South London. His first love was art and he left Bromley Technical High School at 16 to be a commercial artist. But music came a close second. From the mid-1960s, he played in various mod bands and soon had to change his surname to Bowie – to avoid confusion with famous Monkees' star Davy Jones!

THE EARLY YEARS

After many early flops, Bowie made No. 5 with his innovative single, 'Space Oddity' (1969). It told the story of Major Tom, an astronaut who does not want to return to Earth, and earned Bowie an award for 'Astounding Originality' from the UK Songwriters' Guild.

CHANGES

Bowie was beginning to make waves. In 1971 he released 'The Man Who Sold The World', a heavy guitar rock album, followed by 'Hunky Dory'.

Young Bowie as a mod in the '60s.

Bowie also achieved cult status as an actor. In his movie debut, he played a TV-obsessed alien in the bizarre classic, 'The Man Who Fell To Earth' (1976). A string of top parts followed. In 'Merry Christmas Mr Lawrence' (1982), he gave an acclaimed performance as a British army officer in a Japanese prisoner-of-war camp. The following year he resurrected his early alter ego for 'Ziggy Stardust – The Motion Picture' ('83). 'Absolute Beginners' and 'Labyrinth' (both '86) were less successful, but in '88 Bowie was brilliant as Pontius Pilate in Martin Scorcese's controversial film, 'The Last Temptation Of Christ'.

Bowie in 'The Man Who Fell To Earth'.

'Hunky Dory' contained the classics, 'Changes', 'Oh! You Pretty Things' and 'Life On Mars'. It seemed that Bowie had the talent to embrace any musical style with great success.

ALTERED STATES

Bowie's follow-up was the creation of one of his many misfit alter egos, Ziggy Stardust. As Ziggy, Bowie paraded his bisexuality – and taste for wearing dresses. 'The Rise & Fall Of Ziggy Stardust' brought worldwide fame and is now a glitter rock classic. The release of the cleverly-titled 'Aladdin Sane' brought another change of image. It gave him his long-awaited No. 1 hit album, and one of its tracks, 'Drive-In Saturday', made the UK Top 5. Bowie was unstoppable. His next two albums also topped the charts: 'Pin Ups', an album of cover versions, and 'Diamond Dogs', which featured the hit 'Rebel, Rebel'.

Bowie performs as his flamboyant creation, Ziggy Stardust, in the early '70s.

BEYOND THE 1970s

Bowie's success has not diminished. In the 1980s, he enjoyed hit after hit, including 'Let's Dance' and 'This Is Not America'. In '89 Bowie, ever restless, founded a new band, Tin Machine. The band did not do well, but Bowie was soon back on form. With the albums 'Outside' (1995) and 'Earthling' ('97), he explored a more industrial sound, drawing on ambient, techno and jungle influences and proving that – after a quarter of a century – Bowie is still brilliant at reinventing himself.

In 1985, Bowie and Jagger previewed 'Dancing In The Street' at Live Aid.

'Hunky Dory'
December '71
'The Rise & Fall Of Ziggy Stardust'
June '72
'Aladdin Sane'
April '73
'Low'
January '77

'Heroes'
October '77
'Scary Monsters (And Super Creeps)'
September '80
'Singles 1969–1993'
November '93

ERIC CLAPTON

Eric Clapp was born in 1945 in Ripley, Surrey. He was brought up by his grandparents who encouraged his early interest in music. They bought him a guitar and the young Eric started his musical career as a busker, earning pennies on street corners.

'Five Live Yardbirds'
December '64
'Bluesbreakers'
July '66
'Fresh Cream'
December '66
'461 Ocean Boulevard'
September '74
'Just One Night'
April '80
'Timepieces: The Best Of Eric Clapton'
November '82
'The Cream Of Eric Clapton'
September '87

HARD TIMES

Eric didn't stay on the street for long. In 1963, now called Clapton, he formed the Roosters with Tom McGuinness. But success eluded them.

Starving and broke, Clapton joined London's top rhythm and blues (R&B) band, the Yardbirds, in 1964. Their first album, 'The Five Live Yardbirds', was frantic, fast and furious and perfectly captured the band's exciting but erratic stage show. Clapton was soon unhappy about the direction the Yardbirds took. Their chart single, 'For Your Love', was the last straw. Clapton joined John Mayall's Bluesbreakers for half the salary and performed on the classic UK blues album of the same name. But he didn't stay long.

Clapton (centre) felt the Yardbirds were not true to the 'pure' blues he wanted to play.

CREAM

Clapton, bass player Jack Bruce and volatile drummer Ginger Baker, formed arguably the first 'supergroup' – Cream. They had a breathtakingly successful career from 1966 to '68.

After one album with ego-fuelled supergroup, Blind Faith, Clapton craved a quieter life and joined Delaney and Bonnie. After one album with them, Clapton recorded the first of his solo albums, 'Eric Clapton'.

Every Cream album had sales of over $1,000,000.

His wish to be 'just the guitar player' stalled after he wrote and recorded the fabulous 'Layla' with Derek and the Dominoes in 1970, which launched him again into the international spotlight.

BEATING DRUGS

But Clapton's drug addiction nearly killed him. He sold many of his beloved guitars as he spent £1,000 a week on his habit. In 1973 Eric Clapton emerged from the wilderness. A concert in London, organised by his friend Pete Townshend of the Who, was a huge success. Although he was not entirely free from demons – a period of alcoholism followed – Clapton made a steady climb back. Many more successful albums are testaments to his complete recovery and ever-increasing popularity. In 1992 'Unplugged', one of his most successful albums, showed that he has not lost his touch.

Eric, as Derek, made one album with the Dominoes.

Clapton continues to pack out London's biggest venues in the '90s.

PATTI BOYD

Beautiful women have always inspired writers, composers and painters to produce some of their best and most impassioned works. In 1965 the Beatles, then at the height of their fame, made their first film, 'A Hard Day's Night'. A witty and entertaining production, it has a sequence on a train on which the Beatles were travelling to a concert. Fellow passengers included a group of schoolgirl fans. The actress portraying one of them became the inspiration for three beautiful love songs.

The Beatles' George Harrison composed 'Something (In The Way She Moves)' and Eric Clapton wrote 'Layla' and 'Wonderful Tonight' for this attractive woman, Pattie Boyd.

Beatle Harrison's wife, Patti, later married Eric.

The EAGLES

Statistics don't reveal which records are played most often on radio stations all over the world year in, year out, but if they did, the Eagles' 'Hotel California' would surely be close to the top of the list. Recorded in 1976, this beautiful song was a perfect example of band members drawing upon their country and folk music backgrounds and their strong feeling for rock music to create memorable compositions.

BACKING GROUP

The Eagles were formed in 1971 when founder members Glenn Frey and Don Henley worked together backing the acclaimed singer Linda Ronstadt.

Guitarist and singer Frey and drummer Henley soon got together with bass player Randy Meisner and guitarist Bernie Leadon. All had excellent musical pedigrees. David Geffen, the owner of Asylum Records, was impressed by their songwriting skills and offered them a contract.

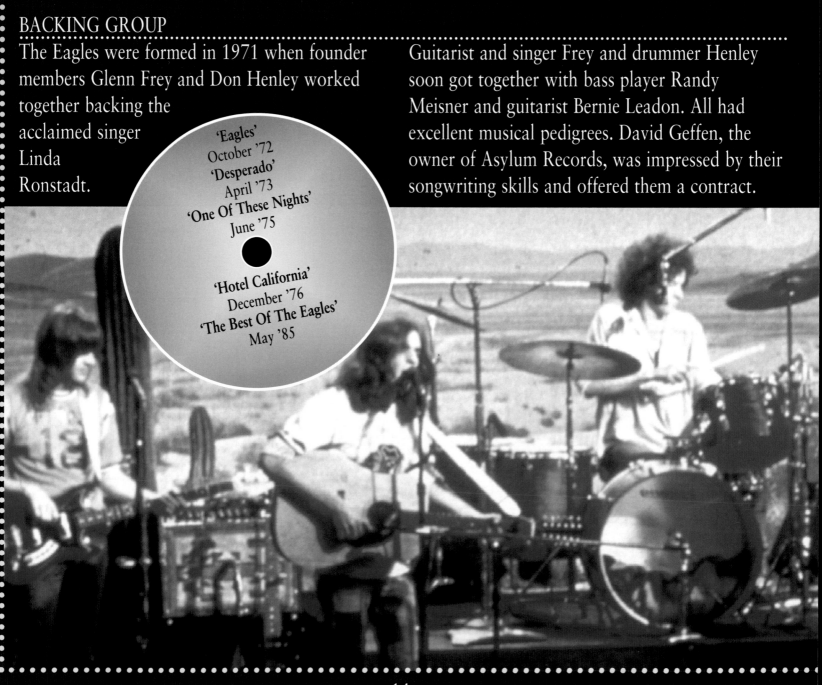

'Eagles'
October '72
'Desperado'
April '73
'One Of These Nights'
June '75

'Hotel California'
December '76
'The Best Of The Eagles'
May '85

14

The Eagles play Wembley Stadium in London.

'Take It Easy' came out in June 1972. By the end of '72, the Eagles had their first two singles and their debut album in the Top 20 and 30 respectively. They parted from Ronstadt but remained close to her.

HOTEL CALIFORNIA

The Eagles recruited Don Felder on slide guitar. Frey said, "He just blew us all away. It was just about the best guitar work we had ever heard". Good sales of their album, 'On The Border', ensured sell-out concerts and the classic, 'One Of These Nights', gave them their first UK hit. 'Lyin' Eyes' and 'Take It To The Limit' charted in the UK too and reached the Top 5 in the USA. Leaden left so guitar player Joe Walsh joined. Walsh was a talented guitarist and songwriter. In 1976 the Eagles released 'Hotel California', an album which for sheer, consistent quality, surpassed everything else they had done. The album and memorable single of the same name went to the top of the charts. 'New Kid In Town', another single from the album, had already made No. 1.

In 1979 Meisner left to go solo and Timothy Schmit replaced him. Although some felt that the Eagles had passed their creative peak by the end of the decade, they had lost none of their commercial touch.

REUNION

The album 'The Long Run' in 1979 sold truckloads, as did 'The Eagles Live' in '80. But the band members wanted to move on and in 1982, members Henley, Frey and 'new boy' Felder, all prolific writers, decided to break up. One of the all-time classic US rock bands was no more. However, band members did get back together for a reunion in the '90s. The project? 'The Hell Freezes Over' tour. The name came from the post-split avowal from Henley and Frey, "This band will only ever tour again when Hell freezes over...!"

'70s' Eagles' concerts sold out instantly.

FLEETWOOD MAC

Fleetwood Mac were formed in London in 1967 by guitarist Peter Greenbaum. Peter, shortening his name to Green, had just left John Mayall's Bluesbreakers. An enormously talented blues guitarist, Green decided to form his own outfit – originally called Peter Green's Fleetwood Mac, but Green didn't like having his name in the band's title. Fleetwood Mac came from the surnames of the rhythm section, drummer Mick Fleetwood and bass player John McVie – but they hit a problem when John McVie wouldn't leave the Bluesbreakers!

McVIE MAKES UP HIS MIND

McVie received a secure income from Mayall. Why swap all that for the risks of joining a totally unknown group? Green hired Bob Brunning instead, fresh from his college band, Five's Company. Fleetwood Mac started rehearsing and recording, preparing for their debut concert at the Windsor Jazz and Blues Festival. They were joined there by second guitarist Jeremy Spencer and the nervous band went down extremely well. Weeks later Brunning stepped aside when McVie decided to take the plunge.

Fleetwood Mac were on their way. Their first album was released in 1967. It was a big success and they toured incessantly in the UK and Europe. But Peter Green left! He was disillusioned with the whole music industry, wanting to give all of the Mac's earnings to charity.

'Peter Green's Fleetwood Mac: Live At The Marquee'
August '67
'Peter Green's Fleetwood Mac'
February '68
'Then Play On'
September '69

'Rumours'
February '77
'Tusk'
October '79
'The Dance'
October '97

Spencer and new guitarist Danny Kirwam also left. The band struggled to survive.

RESCUE
Fleetwood bumped into singer Stevie Nicks and guitarist Lindsey Buckingham. Fleetwood Mac had already recruited McVie's wife Christine, and the five musicians found that their creative chemistry was magical. In 1976, they recorded 'Rumours', a collection of songs documenting the band's personal problems. In the same year the McVies split up, as did Buckingham and Nicks. Fleetwood divorced his wife.

The London Brit Awards.

MAC SPLIT FOR A DECADE
'Rumours' was one of the most successful albums of all time, but the band disintegrated in the late '80s. In 1993 US President Clinton asked them to perform at his inaugural party. Their 'Don't Stop' single had been his campaign song. In 1997 they got together again, 31 years after their first appearance – and in '98 they received a special Brit award for their lifelong contribution to popular music.

PETER GREEN
Mick Fleetwood and John McVie have consistently credited Peter Green for his vision and impressive writing skills. He wrote the band's early hits, 'Albatross', 'Oh Well', 'Man Of The World', 'Black Magic Woman', 'The Green Manalishi' and more.

By 1970, Green's personal life was disintegrating. Drug abuse and a long illness led to his complete withdrawal from the music business. Fleetwood kept in touch but could do nothing to help. But in the mid-'90s Green began a miraculous recovery, performing with his own 'Splinter Group', touring and apparently thoroughly enjoying the experience.

Green goes back on the road in the '90s.

17

JETHRO TULL

The visual image that a band creates is an important factor in their success – or failure. How about trying to promote a band whose front man constantly twists one leg around the other and hops one-legged around the stage, dressed in a long, shabby coat with his uncombed frizzy hair flying madly around? Ian Anderson's choice of instrument was quite bizarre for the time too – the flute.

'This Was'
October '68
'Stand Up'
July '69
'Aqualung'
March '71
'Thick As A Brick'
March '72

'A Passion Play'
July '73
'Twenty Years Of Jethro Tull'
June '88
'The Very Best Of Jethro Tull -
The Anniversary Collection'
May '93

THE MARQUEE

One of Jethro Tull's 'b' sides was 'One For John Gee', a character of the London music scene. The band's appearances at the Marquee were vital to their success. John Gee managed the club and was a benevolent tyrant. Start your set two minutes late and his full wrath would descend. The Marquee saw the very first London performances of the Rolling Stones, the Who, Jimi Hendrix, the Yardbirds and many others. First located in Oxford Street, the Marquee moved to Wardour Street in the '60s and is now in Soho's Dean Street.

The Marquee in Soho's Wardour Street.

LEAVING HOME

Named after an 18th century agriculturalist, Jethro Tull were an innovative and unusual band. Leader Ian Anderson and bass player Glenn Cornick had worked together in a Blackpool band. They joined forces with guitarist Mick Abrahams and his drummer, Clive Bunker and moved to London. They started working on the busy clubs and pubs circuit there.

Anderson initially felt out of his depth. "I'd never been away from home before. It was just like the yokel hitting the city with all his belongings in a knotted handkerchief at the end of a stick."

UNDERGROUND ROCK

They soon secured a contract with Island Records and released the single, 'A Song For Jeffrey'. It was a hit and so was their bluesy album, 'This Was', which featured Anderson's Roland Kirk-inspired flute playing and helped establish underground rock as a musical force. Anderson's eccentric stage presence (he would often perform whilst lying down) made great entertainment and Jethro Tull became a huge concert attraction, finding a following in the USA as 'art-rock'. In 1968 Abrahams left to form Blodwyn Pig and many changes followed. Cornick left in 1970 and Bunker in '71.

Anderson played guitar as well as the flute.

CONCEPT ALBUMS

In 1969 and '70 three Jethro Tull singles entered the UK Top 10 and in '71 the themed album 'Aqualung', accusing the church of damaging man's belief in God, was released. 'Thick As A Brick' and 'A Passion Play' followed. Each effectively contained only one piece of music. The press were critical, although both sold well. Anderson, upset, retired – but not for long.

FOLK ALBUMS

Towards the end of the '70s Jethro Tull's albums became more folk-styled. The band played through the '80s, making their 25th album, 'Catfish Rising' in 1991. Alongside his country squire lifestyle, managing a salmon farm on the Isle of Skye, Anderson still makes a big contribution to the music scene.

Abrahams still plays as Blodwyn Pig.

19

The MOODY BLUES

The Moody Blues began their career as a rhythm and blues band. However, the '70s brought a complete change of direction for the band and their fortunes fluctuated dramatically until their temporary break-up in 1974. Denny Laine, Mike Pinder, Ray Thomas, Graham Edge and Clint Warwick formed the first version of the Moody Blues in Birmingham in 1964.

AN R&B HIT

They moved to London. A residency at the Marquee club followed and an appearance on the influential TV show 'Ready, Steady, Go' led to a contract with the Decca record company. The Moody Blues' second single, released in 1965, with its descending piano introduction, was a hit. 'Go Now' went to the top of the UK charts and made the US Top 10. Their next three singles flopped, although they produced a debut album featuring some excellent original material and rhythm and blues (R&B) covers. Exhausted and disillusioned, Laine and Warwick left the group.

'Brummies' John Lodge and Justin Hayward joined the band. Three flops later, the Moody Blues called a crisis conference. Their R&B phase had just ended.

'The Magnificent Moodies'
July '65
'Days Of Future Passed'
November '67
'On The Threshold Of A Dream'
April '69

'A Question Of Balance'
August '70
'Octave'
June '78
'The Best Of The Moody Blues'
November '84

Early days and a far cry from their supergroup gigs.

NIGHTS IN WHITE SATIN

Hayward wrote 'Nights In White Satin'. Quasi-classical and with obscure, poetic lyrics, the song was a million miles away from their previous material. It crashed into the UK Top 20, their first hit for three years. With the London Festival Orchestra they recorded the album, 'Days Of Future Passed'. It was huge on both sides of the Atlantic.

Six great albums followed, all with a recurring theme. 'The Dream' ('On The Threshold Of A Dream'), 'The Balance' ('A Question Of Balance') and 'My Song' ('Every Good Boy Deserves Favour') were dreams of a better world.

The Moody Blues toured using the revolutionary Mellotron, an organ-like instrument which used tapes to reproduce orchestral sounds on stage. They founded their own record company in 1973 and that year, and again in '79, 'Nights In White Satin' re-entered the US charts.

FOUR YEARS OFF

In 1974 the band members decided to pursue solo careers. They reunited in 1978 to record the excellent album 'Octave'. By the end of the '70s they were unassailable. Although not all their albums

released between 1974 and '93 were huge hits, their concerts have completely sold out at almost every venue they have played for the last two decades.

COLLEGE GIGS

Students in the '70s saw many bands, just by wandering down to their college hall. The college gig circuit drew impressive names. Just imagine you are the student social secretary of a UK university, responsible for booking bands for college concerts. A van pulls up outside containing instruments, amplifiers and four musicians. One of them is Denny Laine. He offers to play a concert that evening for £200. You hesitate. Concerts should really have advance publicity. Who's in the band and what's its name? Paul McCartney and Wings. Missing life on the road after the Beatles broke up, McCartney took Wings all over the country in this way, thrilling countless lucky students.

Denny Laine (left) joined Paul and Linda McCartney in Wings.

VAN MORRISON

Part of the fun of being a teenager is irritating your parents by playing music very loudly in your bedroom. George Ivan, born in Belfast, Northern Ireland found it difficult to rebel in this way, because his parents were playing their music very loudly in the front room! Their impressively huge record collection, including blues, jazz and world music made the Ivan household a very stimulating place to be.

PROFESSIONAL AT 15

The twelve year old Ivan couldn't wait to make some music of his own, although the influences he gained through listening to his parents' music stayed with him. He started to learn the guitar and saxophone and joined a local group. By 15, Ivan had renamed himself Van Morrison, quit school and become a professional musician with the Monarchs. They played rhythm and blues (R&B) and soul music and toured the UK and Europe. Quite a life for a teenager! He released his first single before he left the Monarchs, 'Boozoo Hully Gully'.

THEM

Morrison joined Belfast band the Gamblers. They became Them and Morrison was on his way. 'Here Comes The Night' and 'Baby Please Don't Go' were both hits.

Them appeared on UK TV's 'Ready, Steady, Go' in 1965.

Morrison is a master of the saxophone.

But probably their best known recording from this period (1965) is 'Gloria'.

THEM HIT THE ROAD

Them toured Europe with some of Morrison's greatest heroes. Working with musicians such as Little Walter and Bo Diddley was an education for Van, still barely into his 20s. He toured the West Coast of the USA and worked with an unknown group who later recorded his 'Gloria' with great success – the Doors. The classic Them line-up disbanded upon their return.

'Astral Weeks'
November '68
'Tupelo Honey'
November '71
'The Best Of Van Morrison'
March '90

'The Best Of Van Morrison: Vol 2'
February '93
'Too Long In Exile'
June '93

SOLO SUCCESS

After the success of his album 'Moondance' in 1970 Morrison became a major concert attraction in the USA. Although irritated by the 'star' element of the music business and moody and uncommunicative by nature, Morrison put his heart and soul into his committed performances. 'Tupelo Honey', including love songs for his wife, and 'It's Too Late To Stop Now' – a live album from a 1974 tour of the USA and Europe brought Morrison to the height of his career. After his divorce in 1973 Morrison returned to Ireland for a while. The songs he wrote there appeared on the great 'Veedon Fleece' album.

JOHN LEE HOOKER

In 1917, John Lee Hooker was born in Mississippi, USA. Morrison had heard his wonderful blues music from a very early age and his admiration of Hooker's work increased over the years.

Morrison, himself a superstar in the '80s and '90s, never forgot his early touring experiences with Hooker and in 1993 invited him to duet on the album 'Too Long In Exile'. Morrison had contributed to Hooker's hit album 'Mr. Lucky', released in 1991. It reached No. 3 in the UK charts. Not at all bad for a 74-year-old...!

STILL A STAR

Having released a steady stream of hit albums over 30 years, Van Morrison's career continues to thrive. He has a unique talent and a huge following.

Morrison and Hooker have mutual admiration of very long standing.

PROCOL HARUM

In 1959, five schoolboys formed a rhythm and blues band called the Paramounts and started playing versions of blues and soul music around the pubs and clubs of Southend on England's South coast. Gary Brooker was their singer.

ONE HIT WONDER

In 1962 the Paramounts left school and by '64 their single, 'Poison Ivy', was in the UK Top 40. But in 1966, many flops later, they disbanded. Brooker then teamed up with lyricist Keith Reid. They wrote many songs and advertised for musicians. They renamed themselves the Pinewoods, then Procol Harum (from Latin, meaning 'far from these things').

A WHITER SHADE OF PALE

Reid and Brooker wrote a very unusual song. Based on the classical composer J. S. Bach's 'Suite No. 3 in D Major', better known as the 'Air On A G String', the song had surreal lyrics and a cantata-like part for the organ. It sounded completely different from everything else in the pop charts at the time.

The musicians persuaded influential producer Denny Cordell to record the song. He loved it and used his influence to get the popular pirate radio station, Radio London, to play it round the clock. 'A Whiter Shade Of Pale' went straight to No. 1 in the UK charts and stayed there for six weeks. It entered the US charts, peaking at No. 5. Ex-Paramounts guitarist Robin Trower returned to join Brooker in Procol Harum, with new drummer B. J. Wilson.

'Procol Harum'
December '67
'Shine On Brightly'
December '68
'A Salty Dog'
May '69
'Procol Harum In Concert With The Edmonton Symphony Orchestra'
April '72
'Grand Hotel' March '73
'The Collection'
April '86

Classically-influenced music with state-of-the-art lighting.

In 1967 the new line-up had another Top 10 hit, 'Homburg'. They recorded their first album, 'Procol Harum', and soon became more successful in the USA than the UK. Their second album, 'Shine On Brightly', charted in the USA but not in the UK.

'70s SUCCESS

The '70s brought Procol Harum's greatest success. They played at the huge Atlanta and Isle of Wight pop festivals and in 1972 released their sixth album, recorded live in Canada with the Edmonton Symphony Orchestra. It sold a million copies, earning a gold disc. The single, 'Conquistador', entered the US Top 20 in July of that year. With yet another line-up the band toured the world from 1973 to '77, to great acclaim.

'70s FASHION FAILURES

While Procol Harum resembled medieval pageboys, their fans wore a mix of fashions that have earned the '70s the adjective, 'tasteless'. Knee high boots, platform soled, were worn with very long and tight flared loons (cotton trousers) or jeans. Hot pants were the new invention for girls. Long hair or afro perms were for everyone, with facial hair too for boys. T-shirts were tight, tie-dyed or plain. Later came the despised tank top, maybe even striped, and worn over puffy-sleeved shirts! Dungarees were fashion wear for young adults for the first time – but only briefly. Skirts could be knee-length, mid-calf or 'maxi', a term coined as the opposite of the '60s mini.

Nostalgia, too, was rife with fashions taken from movies such as 'The Godfather' and 'The Great Gatsby'.

They recorded four more albums, including the excellent 'Grand Hotel'. But by June 1977, the band found themselves unable to compete with the burgeoning punk and new wave scene and decided to call it a day. The members went their different (and extremely successful) ways. Procol Harum wasn't quite finished however. In 1991 they reformed with most of the original members and made the creditable but commercially unsuccessful album, 'The Prodigal Stranger'.

Boob tubes and skin-tight lurex flares were popular fashion items in '70s discos.

The SEX PISTOLS

The Sex Pistols were originally formed in 1975 by Steve Jones, Paul Cook and Glen Matlock. They were then known as the Swankers. Their manager, Malcolm McLaren, introduced them to John Lydon. Lydon changed his name to Johnny Rotten and the Swankers became the Sex Pistols.

ANARCHISTS

The band projected an aggressive, confrontational image. Although not great musicians, they wrought an enormous influence on rock 'n' roll and the music industry. They railed against authority, flaunted their drug and alcohol addiction and made headlines. They persuaded the EMI record company to pay a £40,000 advance and released a single, 'Anarchy In The UK'. They hijacked a TV chat show, arguing with presenter Bill Grundy and offending viewers with their obscene language. The record was banned. EMI promptly dropped the Sex Pistols but the group kept their cash advance. The A&M company signed them up a month later in March 1977.

'Never Mind The B*******, Here's The Sex Pistols'
November '77
'The Great Rock 'n' Roll Swindle'
March '79

'The Best And The Rest Of The Sex Pistols'
February '96

The archetypal punk wore a Mohican haircut but any variety of spiky, coloured hair sculpture would do.

VICIOUS JOINS

The band sacked Matlock for being too 'nice' and brought in a musician who better fitted the violent image they wanted to project – John Simon Ritchie, a drug addict and would-be bass player. Ritchie changed his name to Sid Vicious. His aggressive nature provoked countless fights on and off stage. When, tragically, he blinded a member of the audience at a Pistol's gig by hurling a glass into the crowd, A&M dropped the band, losing their £75,000 advance. The Pistols had signed their contract outside Buckingham Palace just one week earlier.

VIRGIN DEAL

Virgin took them on next – this time for £15,000. The single, 'God Save The Queen', ranted against the British monarchy. Banned, it went to No. 2 in the UK charts. In the same year their album, 'Never Mind The B*******', Here's The Sex Pistols', made No. 1 in the UK.

THE END

After a shambolic US tour, Rotten announced the break-up of the band. In October 1978, Vicious allegedly murdered his girlfriend in New York. By February 1979 he was dead himself, from a heroin overdose. The Sex Pistols were no more but their influence survives in the music of bands like Nirvana and Guns N' Roses.

PUNK

As a fashion movement punk, with its bin liners, safety pins, chains and spiky hairdos had some followers and lots of press. As a music form it became a dominant force in rock culture. UK teenagers viewed punk as a Brave New Dawn, the overthrowing of authority, a celebration of anarchy.

In the USA punk's audience was small, perhaps because its ethos was too removed from the American Dream. Working class heroes have to make good – pretending low birth wasn't on. New York's New Wave came close, with the New York Dolls and Velvet Underground.

Punk guru Malcolm McLaren also briefly managed the New York Dolls.

ROD STEWART

For a while it looked as if Roderick David Stewart, born in 1945 in London, would appear in the UK's stadiums as a football hero. He signed as an apprentice for Brentford Football Club and longed to make a career in the sport he loved so passionately. But his equally fervent involvement with blues and soul music took precedence.

FIRST SUCCESSES

In the '60s, a 'blues boom' was beginning to flourish in the UK. Blues bands packed the pubs and clubs with their fans. Rod Stewart's gravelly, soulful voice ensured him a place in the movement.

After stints as harmonica player and vocalist with three unsuccessful bands, Stewart was invited by the already successful Jeff Beck to join his new band. Beck had played in the Yardbirds with guitarist Jimmy Page (who later gained superstar status with the band, Led Zeppelin) but wanted to create his own group. The Jeff Beck Group made two excellent albums, 'Truth' and 'Beck-Ola', but when Beck hired two members of the US band Vanilla Fudge, Stewart decided that he'd had enough.

'An Old Raincoat
Won't Ever Let You Down'
February '70
'Gasoline Alley'
September '70
'Every Picture Tells A Story'
July '71

'Atlantic Crossing' August '75
'A Night On The Town'
June '76
'The Best Of Rod Stewart'
Vol 1 June '77
Vol 2 August '77

THE FACES

Life then got complicated. No sooner had he signed a contract as a solo artist in 1969, than Stewart joined yet another band, the Faces. Born out of the ashes of the brilliant Small Faces, they cheerfully undertook a chaotic life on the road. Rod could out-party them all, but amazingly found time to record both as a solo artist and as a 'Face'. His solo career brought him infinitely greater rewards.

Out came 'An Old Raincoat Won't Ever Let You Down'. It wasn't a hit, but it certainly made people sit up and listen. In 1970 his second album, 'Gasoline Alley', scraped into the Top 50.

Stewart's stint with Jeff Beck was short.

GLAM ROCK

The '70s saw the emergence of 'glam rock'. Outrageous glitter and lurex-laden stage costumes, crazy haircuts and customised guitars enhanced the careers of many bands.

Ironically, many glam rock bands featured seasoned and accomplished performers who adopted their extravagant poses for entirely commercial reasons.

David Bowie was the master of glam in the early '70s, reinventing himself in the vanguard of each new fashion. Bands like Slade, the Sweet and T. Rex followed suit.

First a mod, then a hippie, Marc Bolan of T. Rex became a glam rocker.

MAGGIE MAY

But in July 1971 his stunning version of the traditional song, 'Maggie May', topped the singles charts. His third album, 'Every Picture Tells A Story', also reached No. 1 on the album charts. Part of the charm of all three albums was their shambolic, under-rehearsed, we're-all-having-a-good-time feel. Stewart was still having fun on the road with the party-loving Faces and continued to record with them, although their albums were not as successful as his own. In August 1972, another solo single made the No. 1 spot. 'You Wear It Well' sounded a lot like 'Maggie May', but the similarity probably helped its success.

Stewart embraced the glam rock look and has always taken care over his image.

A SOLO CAREER

Stewart decided to concentrate on the solo side of things. He began to record more blatantly commercial songs, some of them unashamedly sexist.

Between 1972 and '95 he had 28 singles and 15 of his albums in the Top 20. His decision to sing for his supper rather than kick a ball around for Brentford F.C. had certainly paid off!

GAZETTEER

The visual image which bands choose to project has always been a very significant factor in their success or failure. In an ideal world, only the music would ever count, but impressionable young fans have always set great store by the way their heroes look, as well as sound. The Bay City Rollers were heavily dependent on their costumes of short, baggy tartan trousers and waist-length jackets but they didn't have many imitators, except among their fans.

Slade

GLAM ROCK

The incredibly theatrical glam rock performers took image to the extreme but while many, Queen, T. Rex and Elton John to name just a few, were producing excellent records, the quality of some 'glam rock' music was a secondary consideration. Image was all!

The Clash

PUNK

However, the punk music explosion opened the door to many bands who chose to challenge the establishment rather than just pose. In the UK the Sex Pistols wanted to shock, as had the Prime Movers and the Stooges, both featuring Iggy Pop, and MC5 in the USA, but other bands chose to be subversive and critical in a more subtle way.

The Stranglers

NEW WAVE

The Stranglers, the Jam, the Clash, Elvis Costello and many other 'new wave' bands brought sensitive musical skills to their political statements. Lou Reed kept the flag flying for US new wave as did the interesting and provoking Blondie, Ultravox, the Ramones and Talking Heads.

COUNTRY AND WESTERN

Dolly Parton

Dolly Parton also enjoyed huge commercial success during the '70s, spearheading a new generation of fine country and western performers who lovingly carried on the tradition established by their legendary predecessors, including Merle Travis, Hank Williams and many more. Never as popular in the UK as in the USA, the new breed of country performers sold many millions of records all over the world.

TEENYBOPPER HEROES

The Bay City Rollers

While Bay City Roller-instigated 'Rollermania' ran riot in the UK, in the USA the TV sitcom, 'The Partridge Family', took over where the Monkees left off in the '60s. David Cassidy became the heartthrob of millions of teenage, and younger, girls and had many hits. The Osmonds too, first with Donny and later with 'Little' Jimmy, kept a consistent presence in the charts through the early '70s. But even more prolific than these were the Jackson 5, fronted by eleven-year-old Michael, who were rarely out of the charts for the entire decade – and, in the case of Michael, ever since.

POPULAR MUSIC MOVES EVER ONWARDS

Lou Reed

All in all, the '70s turned out to be a rich and exciting time for the development of popular music. The '60s were indeed a hard act to follow, but the following decade produced a wide variety of influential performers.

Blondie

INDEX

PHOTOGRAPHIC CREDITS *Abbreviations: t-top, m-middle, b-bottom, r-right, l-left, c-centre.*
Front cover c - M. Prior/Redferns. Cover bl & bm, 5, 4-5, 8-9, 23, 26t & bl, 27bl, 29t & 31t - Richie Aaron/Redferns. Cover br - G. Terrell/Redferns. 5, 10br, 12t & 13b - M. Hutson/Redferns. 6t, 8 both, 19b, 24t & 28l - Glen A Baker Archives/Redferns. 6b - P. Ford. 6-7, 12b, 13t & 24-25 - Michael Ochs Archives/Redferns. 7 both, 10bl, 11t, 18b, 19m, 20-21, 21b, 22-23, 25b, 29br, 31m & b - Redferns. 9t, 11b, 14-15, 20t, 22t, 27br & 30t - RB/Redferns. 9b - Paramount Pictures (courtesy Kobal). 10t, 15b, 16l, 23b & 30m - E. Roberts/Redferns. 11m - EMI films (courtesy Kobal). 13m - G. Wiltshire/Redferns. 14t - Gems/Redferns. 15t & 17m - R. Parkin/Redferns. 16r & 17b - Retna. 17t - J. Marshall. 18t, 18-19, 19t & 28r - D. Ellis/Redferns. 21t - CA/Redferns. 22b - S & G/Redferns. 25t - E. Landy/Redferns. 26br & 27t - E. Echenberg/Redferns. 29bl - K. Morris/Redferns. 30b - F. Costello/Redferns.